STEPPING INTO DISCIPLESHIP
Our Journey Begins

STEPPING INTO DISCIPLESHIP
Our Journey Begins

By Mary Venable–Vaughn

ReadersMagnet, LLC

STEPPING INTO DISCIPLESHIP: Our Journey Begins
Copyright © 2022 by Mary Venable–Vaughn

Published in the United States of America

ISBN   Paperback: 978-1-958030-56-1
ISBN   eBook: 978-1-958030-57-8

All rights reserved. No part of this publication may be reproduced, stored in a retrieval system or transmitted in any way by any means, electronic, mechanical, photocopy, recording or otherwise without the prior permission of the author except as provided by USA copyright law. The opinions expressed by the author are not necessarily those of ReadersMagnet, LLC.

ReadersMagnet, LLC
10620 Treena Street, Suite 230 | San Diego, California, 92131 USA
1.619. 354. 2643 | www.readersmagnet.com

Book design copyright © 2022 by ReadersMagnet, LLC. All rights reserved.

Cover design by Ericka Obando
Interior design by Daniel Lopez
Revised 2022

Dedication

I am dedicating this book to all the disciple makers that helped me along my Christian journey and took the time to plant seeds of love, joy and hope in my life. The Holy Spirit was my inspiration to write this book in 2011. But, in 2013, the unthinkable happened, I was about 60% finished with my manuscript when my computer crashed and I lost it all. Starting over has been a test of my faith and dedication, but God showed me that He is still in the miracle business and He is alive and well.

I thank God that I married my soulmate, Emmanuel Vaughn, Sr., he has been very supportive of me in all my projects. I thank God that I have a husband that is loving, caring and giving, he has made my life full of joy. He inspires me to dream, his favorite saying is "What you dare to dream, dare to do!"

Testimony

On June 3, 2014, I had a heart attack and had to have bypass surgery. One of my heart's arteries was 100% blocked. During traditional heart bypass surgery, a surgeon makes an incision (about 6 to 8 inches) down the center of your sternum (breastbone) to get direct access to your heart. You are connected to a heart-lung bypass machine, which allows for circulation of blood throughout your body during surgery. The heart is stopped and the surgeon then performs the bypass procedure described above. The heart is generally stopped for about 30-90 minutes of the 4-5 hour surgery. After surgery, the surgeon closes the breastbone with special sternal wires and the chest with special internal or traditional external stitches.

The strangest thing about my surgery is that no incision was made in my chest, I was not put on a heart-lung bypass machine, no human hands touched my heart and the surgery only took 3-5 minutes. In that 3-5 minutes God stopped my heart, placed two blood vessels from the good side of my heart to feed blood to the side of the blocked artery. Let me go back and explain what happened before I went to the hospital. My husband and I had gone to the beach for a morning walk, we walked for about an hour and we were headed back to the car in the parking lot. As we were walking up the hill to the parking lot, I began to feel faint, I said to my husband "Let's hurry to the car, because I feel like I am going to faint" As I sat down in the car everything went black. When I regained consciousness, my husband was in a state of shock and I was wondering why he was terrified when I had just fainted. We went home and my husband called 911. I found out later that I had stopped breathing and my husband gave me

CPR. The paramedic said that all my vital signs were good, but because I was so weak, I should go to the hospital and get checked out. So I did! As we were riding to the hospital in the ambulance the paramedic was humming a song, I said to him, "I know that song", "It is well with my soul", he said "yes" and began to tell me the background of the writing of the song. At that point I knew in my spirit that I would recover it was God's message to me. On Tuesday morning the hospital did a EKG and blood test and asked me if I was having any pain, I said "No!" and they told me that I was having a heart attack. I said "ok, but I feel fine." So on Thursday my heart doctor ordered an Angiography. Angiography is performed by inserting a catheter into a groin blood vessel and feeding it up into the heart. Dye is then injected, which fills the blood vessels the supply the heart. A type of x-ray is used to take pictures of the dye-filled vessels, which reveals any narrowing or blockage in the blood vessel system. Well, I have an artery that is 100% blocked, and then he noticed something spectacular, two blood vessels that were going straight across my heart. He called my husband into the x-ray room to show him the blood vessels. He said "he has never seen anything like that in his life, he also said "you must know somebody" because the surgery had already been done, there was nothing else they could do! Praise God! It is done! By the Master's hand! My husband was amazed, God is still performing miracles, I was released from the hospital on Friday morning and I was able to attended an NAACP Awards Banquet where my husband was presented with the Medgar Evers Award. How many people do you know that have heart bypass surgery and in three days are able to attend a banquet, it had to be God! This event in my life has inspired me to do many things, one is to finish writing this book "Stepping Into Discipleship" Our Journey Begins" because God needs more disciples working and saving souls for Him. The Holy Spirit inspired me to finish this book to let people know that God is alive and well, still performing miracles every day, you may be next!

INTRODUCTION

THE JOURNEY

"We have not received the spirit of the world but the Spirit who is from God, so that we may understand what God has freely given us." 1Corinthians 2:12 (NIV) In life we have to make many decisions about which roads in life we will travel, will we walk down the road on the right or will we walk down the road on the left or just walk straight down the middle road? We have to make choices every day to follow God or follow Satan! From the beginning of humankind, God has been directing us to follow Him, but sometimes we choose to go in the wrong direction. God sent Jesus down to earth to live among us and to experience the life that His people live every day. Jesus died on the cross for our sins to provide us with a second chance to get it right. The day we accepted Jesus in our lives as our Lord and Savior, He gave us the gift of sanctification. If we follow this process we can thrive to be more like Jesus Christ, becoming a disciple of God, with the determination to keep our eyes on the prize, Jesus Christ. God wants us to know what He gave to us when He went to Calvary, the Holy Spirit! One of the responsibilities of the Holy Spirit is to reveal God's plan for our lives to us. If we seek

the Holy Spirit with all our heart, he will reveal God's plan to us and we can become a disciple for God. We have started many journeys in our lives, some we have finished and some we have not, but this is the most important journey you will ever be on. Will you finish this journey? The choice is yours! Taking this journey will start you on the road to becoming a disciple of Jesus Christ. You might ask yourself what is a disciple? What we learn first is that a disciple is a person who accepts and assists in spreading the doctrines of a person. But, a Christian disciple is a person who accepts and assists in the spreading of the good news of Jesus Christ. I looked on Answers.com and it stated that the process of making disciples can and probably will take a person's whole lifetime to achieve.

Our mission on earth, should you decide to take it, is to win souls for Christ, we are His ambassadors and we need to do His will and do it His way. As stated in 2 Corinthians 5:20, *"We are therefore Christ's ambassadors, as though God were making his appeal through us. We implore you on Christ's behalf: Be reconciled to God."* (NIV) Scripture tells us that Christ has commanded us to become disciples for Him, and then to go out and make disciples for Him. If we chose the road that leads to Christ, He will love and protect us and we will join Him in that great getting up morning. But if we take the road that leads to sin, our lives will be full of roadblocks and detours. With God being our father He will always show us the roads back to Him and if we ask for forgiveness of our sins, He is waiting to welcome you back into the family.

To be a disciple of Christ you will need to work to obtain the Fruits of the Spirit in your life. God wants you to be a fruitful Christian following Him, but if you are not a fruitful Christian the Holy Spirit can work with and in your life to make you a disciple of Christ.

What does it mean to be a Fruitful Christian? As stated on answers.com, "A fruitful Christian must be able to show progress in their walk with God." Just as a baby learns to walk and gets better and better at it, so it is with Christians that work to get the Fruit of the Spirit in their life. We learn to walk spiritually with God as we obey what His word tells us. Another measure of fruit is how much we let God lead our lives. The Oxford Dictionary states fruitful as "producing good results, successful; beneficial. God wants all His children to live fruitful lives and to strive to be more like Christ. We look at the world today and we can see how society is heading in the wrong direction. I am saddened by the state that our world is in. Look at any news station today, police shootings of unarmed black men and women, gang shooting, family shooting, missing children, people just seem to be losing their mind, the killing of thousands of women, men, and children with deadly chemicals, drive-by shootings with no regard for the safety of women or children. Is our world changing into a Sodom and Gomera? It is time that we start getting our lives in order, God is coming soon, we don't know the time or the date, but the Bible talks about these end times in the Book of Revelations, Luke, etc.

COVID-19 has changed the world and the way we live in it. So many people have died, and families are in a state of turmoil. I must ask myself this question, "Is this God's way of bringing us back to Him?" I am not saying that God is letting people die, because that is a choice that people are making on their own. God has provided us with the vaccine to keep us healthy, but people are not getting vaccinated. Maybe we need to focus on God!

In the world today we have to deal with all kinds of people and conditions. COVID-19, women's rights, gay rights, senior citizen rights, your rights, my rights, everybody got rights. It is almost too much to deal with on a daily basis. If it was not for the love of God, we would all be nuts. God is the anchor that we need to hold onto, God keeps us sane in this insane world that we live in. God has provided everything that we need to live a loving, fulfilling, and happy life. We just have to open the door and let the Holy Spirit into our hearts. We have to invite the Holy Spirit into our hearts because the Holy Spirit will not come into our hearts unless asked.

As we read the Bible, God will open our eyes to the many incredible visions that He has given to the Holy Spirit to lead us in the right direction. The bible is our instructional guide for living a fruitful life. Let's take a look at what Galatians 5:16-18(MSG) tells us *"My counsel is this: Live freely, animated and motivated by God's Spirit. Then you won't feed the compulsions of selfishness. For there is a root of sinful self-interest in us that is at odds with a free spirit, just as the free spirit is incompatible with selfishness. These two ways of life are antithetical so that you cannot live at times one way and at times another way according to how you feel on any given day. Why don't you choose to be led by the Spirit and so escape the erratic compulsions of a lawless dominated existence?"* This scripture tells us to decide about who we want to follow, the spirit (fruitful) or the flesh (fruitless)?

Christ asks us to become disciples for Him, stating *"Go ye therefore and make disciples of all the nations, baptizing them into the name of the Father, and of the Son, and of the Holy Spirit: teaching them to observe all things whatsoever I commanded you: and lo, I am with you always, even unto the end of the world".* Matthew 28:19-20(KJV). But before we can make disciples, we must be disciples!

The Bible states: *"Study to shew thyself approved unto God, a workman that needed not to be ashamed, rightly dividing the word of truth."* 2Timothy 2:15(KJV)

The more you apply yourself to the word of God, the more God will be present in your life.

I pray that this book will become a useful tool for you to use in growing in your ministry and a guide for Stepping into Discipleship—Our Journey Begins.

Table of Contents

DEDICATION v
TESTIMONY v
INTRODUCTION ix

CHAPTER ONE	Our Journey Begins – Stepping into God's Gifts	1
CHAPTER TWO	Stepping Into Discipleship – Study to Show Thyself Approved	17
CHAPTER THREE	Mentoring – Godly Advice	67
CHAPTER FOUR	Walking the Walk – God's Way	73
CHAPTER FIVE	Stepping into Discipleship	79

REFERENCES 81

CHAPTER 1

Our Journey Begins – Stepping into God's Gifts

For almost 3 years we have been living with the fear of COVID-19 and now the other viruses. We have learned a new way of living, it has been about three years that we have had to stay at home, avoid crowds, businesses closing, and attending our Sunday Service on a virtual platform. The children staying at home taking classes on the computer, parents working from home, this has been a season that we had to find ways to get along with family members. But more than ever, we have called on God, some for the first time in their lives, to help our families and keep them safe. We have been praying more than ever before, we have lost family members to COVID-19. We have grieved because we could not say goodbye in a way that we had been a custom to an attending funeral services on zoom, this was so impersonal and made our hearts sad. Then just when we thought it was safe to socialize again, with the development of the vaccine, the new verse is attacking the unvaccinated people and the hospitals are filling up again. It would be nice if everyone would get on the same page and get vaccinated. I believe that God gave the scientist the knowledge to make the vaccine to help cure the people. But if you do not have a relationship with God, then you can't see the wonders of His work.

We are going into the year 2022, the virus is still killing people. Why? Because people are not getting vaccinated. The unvaccinated are infecting other people. When is this going to end? I think it will end, when God feels that we have learned what He has been trying to teach us.

Back in the day, when babies were born the doctor would slap them on their rear ends, they would cry and life began. But our journey really begins before this, starting when we are first conceived in our mother's womb, God started forming our bodies, mind, and spirit. The process of learning begins while we are in our mother's womb. How many times have you stated or heard someone say "that child has been here before" I believe that the Holy Spirit talks to us, preparing us for this life before we are born. Our parents, friends, family, and even strangers all take part in planting a seed that starts to shape our character and as we grow we learn right from wrong and good from evil.

God loved us so much that He made us just a little lower than the angels and gave us the ability to choose between good and evil. As we grow in our knowledge of God and develop a relationship with Him, we begin to understand God's plan for our life. God sent His only Son to earth, to learn about the people He had created and loved. Jesus was perfect in every way and God sent Jesus to help us, He did this for us. Before Jesus went to the cross, He let us know that He would not leave us alone. He would send us a comforter the Holy Spirit.

Do you know "What God's Plan is for your life? That's a good question, I am still on my journey to understand God's Plan for my life. But it all starts with you and me! I know that God has His hands on my life and your life.

God has commissioned us: *"Jesus, undeterred, went right ahead and gave his charge: "God authorized and commanded me to commission you: Go out and train everyone you meet, far and near, in this way of life, marking them by baptism in the threefold name: Father, Son, and Holy Spirit. Then instruct them in the practice of all I have commanded you. I'll be with you as you do this, day after day after day, right up to the end of the age."* Matthew 28:19-20(MSG). Think about it, what does this scripture say to you?

God wants us to make disciples, but first, we need to make sure that we are disciples of Jesus Christ, trained and equipped. Jesus, gave us marching orders, to teach others about the goodness of God. We must not be afraid of our sisters and brothers; we must teach them about the love of Jesus Christ. We must be bold and go into areas that are out of our comfort zone. If God tells us to go, He will protect us from any hurt, harm, or danger.

But before we GO, we need to prepare our spirit, so when people meet us they will know that we are disciples of God, we need to work with the Holy Spirit, to help us incorporate the Fruit of the Spirits in our lives. God will prepare us for the purpose He has for us, but we must do our part, you have heard that old saying "faith without works is dead". Also as stated in 1Corinthians 12:1-11(MSG) *"What I want to talk about now is the various ways God's Spirit gets worked into our lives. This is complex and often misunderstood, but I want you to be informed and knowledgeable. Remember how you were when you didn't know God, led from one phony god to another, never knowing what you were doing, just doing it because everybody else did it? It's different in this life. God wants us to use our intelligence, to seek to understand as well as we can. For instance, by using your heads, you know perfectly well that the Spirit of God would never prompt anyone to say "Jesus be damned!" Nor would anyone be inclined to say "Jesus is Master!" without the insight of the Holy Spirit.*

God's various gifts are handed out everywhere, but they all originate in God's Spirit. God's various ministries are carried out everywhere, but they all originate in God's Spirit. God's various expressions of power are in action everywhere, but God himself is behind it all. Each person is given something to do that shows who God is: Everyone gets in on it, everyone benefits. All kinds of things are handed out by the Spirit and to all kinds of people! The variety is wonderful: wise counsel, clear understanding, simple trust, healing the sick, miraculous acts, proclamation, distinguishing between spirits, tongues, and interpretation of tongues. All these gifts have a common origin but are handed out one by one by the one Spirit of God. He decides who gets what, and when.

When we are born God has a purpose for our lives, as we grow our parents, family and friends plant seeds in our lives, some could be good seeds and some could be bad seeds. As we get older we decide which seeds we will keep and which ones we will discard. God will mold us into the people that he wants us to become, God has also given us free will to choose which direction we will go, He has given us the Holy Spirit to consult with us and we need to be opened minded to receive the advice that the Holy Spirit has for us.

It is hard work being a disciple of God! You have to be aware of what you say and how you say it. The words out of your mouth may build someone up or tear someone down. The bible states *"Do not let any unwholesome talk come out of your mouths, but only what is helpful for building others up according to their needs, that it may benefit those who listen."* Ephesians 4:29(NIV)

Life's are destroyed every day by thoughtless words, the tongue is a deadly weapon baby Christians, ranging from ages 2 to 102 years old are looking for you to help build them up and fed them the word of God. They are looking for the Christ in your life, then it happens, your name was left off the program or they didn't give you credit for the work you did or someone didn't speak to you or better still in the Pastor's sermon, it sounded like he was talking about you or someone sat in your seat at church, that is your pew! You forgot that people are watching you and then you stepped from under the umbrella of God's love! Instead of going to that person that you think offended you and talking to them in private, you want everyone to know that you told that person off. You talk down the Pastor, the church, and the people, in that moment of self-indulgence you may have turned a person or persons away from Christ. That person thought you were a Christian, a forgiving Christian because they believed what you had been telling them about being a Christian disciple, now they see you as a phony Christian, talking the talk, but not walking the walk.

Think back to the beginning of your Christian walk, how many times did someone you thought was a Christian, words or action destroyed or delayed your Christian walk? Because you were a baby Christian and you didn't know that you should follow Christ, not man or woman. I am a witness, when I was about 25 years old and going to a church that I grew up in, with my Family of 5 generations. At that time I was just a churchgoer, I had not developed a relationship with God, I knew of God but didn't understand that God is the only one you should put on a pedal. I had put the Pastor on a pedal right up there with God. So when the mess started in church about the Pastor and several of the women in the church, I was devastated! How can the Pastor that talks to God and preaches His word be an adulterer? I left the church and my belief in God decreased, I begin to question everything that the Pastor had done because he was a sinner. I asked myself is my marriage legal? What about my children's Baptism? I had all these questions and no answers. It took me years before I found my way back to church. When I learned that there was a new pastor at my home church, I asked to talk to him and he explained to me that pastors are people too. They make mistakes and can be sinners and that the person that I should have had on the pedal was God. He is the only one that can't let you down, this was the beginning of my building a relationship with God. What if I had never talked to the new pastor, I had my faith in man and not God! Thanks be to God that He led me to the right person. For five years I was out in the wilderness, angry, hurt and confused, I am so happy that I found my way back to God. But how many baby Christians are hurt by pastors or people in the church and never find their way back to God?

Today's generation lives for the moment, they don't know God and they are not looking for Him. God is not real to them! How do we start to fix this problem? We start with ourselves and then one person at a time to bring them to Christ and making them a disciple.

As we grow in our faith and trusting God, more will be asked of us. When we are not willing to take that next step in our learning process, we are no longer considered a disciple! When Jesus asks us to do something and we say no, we throw a wrench in the process, to obey God is to make sacrifices.

The following verses tell us of the wonderful things that we have received from Jesus Christ dying on the cross for us. These blessings were given to us free of charge; some of us don't even know that we have received redemption, righteousness, and sanctification. Hebrews 10:14 – 18 states, *"Every priest goes to work at the altar each day, offers the same old sacrifices year in, year out, and never makes a* dent in the sin problem. As a priest, Christ made a single sacrifice for sins, and that was it! Then he sat down right beside God and waited for his enemies to cave in. It was a perfect sacrifice by a perfect person to perfect some very imperfect people. By that single offering, he did everything that needed to be done for everyone who takes part in the purifying process. The Holy Spirit confirms this: This new plan I'm making with Israel isn't going to be written on paper, isn't going to be chiseled in stone; This time "I'm writing out the plan in them, carving it on the lining of their hearts." He concludes, I'll forever wipe the slate clean of their sins. Once sins are taken care of for good, there's no longer any need to offer sacrifices for them." (MSG)

These were the commandments that God gave us to live our life by, but Christians have gotten so relaxed in keeping God's laws, that every day on the news we hear about raping, killings, stealing, the world is going crazy with the lust of the flesh and crimes. But the good news is that there is a price to pay if we look at Hebrews 10: 26 – 31 *"If we give up and turn our backs on all we've learned, all we've been given, all the truth we now know, we repudiate Christ's sacrifice and are left on our own to face the Judgment—and a mighty fierce judgment it will be! If the penalty for breaking the law of Moses is physical death, what do you think will happen if you turn on God's Son, spit on the sacrifice that made you whole, and insult this most gracious Spirit? This is no light matter. God has warned us that he'll *hold us to account and make us pay. He was quite explicit: "Vengeance is mine, and I won't overlook a thing" and "God will judge his people." Nobody's getting by with anything, believe me."* (MSG) This is a hard judgment; we need to make sure that we are living the life that God has planned for us.

We are God's people and He loves us very much, so much that He wants us to be like His son Jesus Christ, He wants to start the sanctification process in our lives. The day we accepted Jesus Christ as our Lord and Savior was the beginning of our sanctification process. When we gave our lives to God the process started Hebrews 2:10-13 states *"It makes good sense that the God who got everything started and keeps everything going now completes the work by making the Salvation Pioneer perfect through suffering as he leads all these people to glory. Since the One who saves and those who are saved have a common origin, Jesus doesn't hesitate to treat them as family, saying, I'll tell my good friends, my brothers and sisters, all I know about you; I'll join them in worship and praise to you. Again, he puts himself in the same family circle when he says, Even I live by placing my trust in God. And yet again, I'm here with the children God gave me."* (MSG)

Sanctification is a process that means to be set apart, God wants us to be Holy like Him, God wants us to have a close relationship with him. How can we get a closer relationship with God? By entering into the sanctification process with the Holy Spirit. First, we need to forget all our old ways, 1Peter 1:13–16 states *"So roll up your sleeves, put your mind in gear, be ready to receive the gift that's coming when Jesus arrives. Don't lazily slip back into those old grooves of evil, doing just what you feel like doing. You didn't know any better than; you do now. As obedient children, let yourselves be pulled into a way of life shaped by God's life, a life energetic and blazing with holiness. God said, "I am holy; you be holy."* (MSG)

The sanctification process starts from the inside out, changing how you think and feel. God looks at our spirit, not how we look on the outside John 14:25-27 states *"I'm telling you these things while I'm still living with you. The Friend, the Holy Spirit whom the Father will send at my request, will make everything plain to you. He will remind you of all the things I have told you. I'm leaving you well and whole. That's my parting gift to you. Peace. I don't leave you the way you're used to being left—feeling abandoned, bereft. So don't be upset. Don't be distraught."* (MSG) We get a better understanding of what is desired of us in the sanctification process, love is the beginning and without love, there is no joy or peace. God is love and without God, you have a fruitless life.

God is the father of us all, as a good father, He wants the best for us, He gave us the Holy Spirit to implant in us the Fruit of the Spirit.

Being a fruitful Christian in God's sight pleases Him. What if we decide not to follow the Holy Spirit and don't receive the Fruit of the Spirit in our lives? Will that make us fruitless Christians?

What is a fruitless Christian? As defined at Dictionary.com, Fruitless is useless, unproductive; without results or success. If we are not trying to live our lives the way God wants us to, then we are living our life the way we want without God. The bible tells us that trying to have things our way all the time is selfish and self-serving, as stated in Galatians 5:19-21(MSG) *"It is obvious what kind of life develops out of trying to get your own way all the time: repetitive, loveless, cheap sex; a stinking accumulation of mental and emotional garbage; frenzied and joyless grabs for happiness; trinket gods; magic-show religion; paranoid loneliness; cutthroat competition; all-consuming-yet-never-satisfied wants; a brutal temper; impotence to love or be loved; divided homes and divided lives; small-minded and lopsided pursuits; the vicious habit of depersonalizing everyone into a rival; uncontrolled and uncontrollable addictions; ugly parodies of community. I could go on. This isn't the first time I have warned you, you know. If you use your freedom this way, you will not inherit God's kingdom." (MSG)* Inheriting God's kingdom is the prize that we all seek to achieve.

As I look back over my life I can see where God's hand has guided me when I have strayed from God's grace. God loved me enough to put me back on the right road. God has always been right there when I needed Him and He will be there for you if you believe. If you don't have a relationship with God, you still have missed the boat, because having a relationship with God is the most important relationship you can have in your life. You want someone that will love you unconditionally, pick you up when you are down, make a way out of no way, then God is waiting for you to invite Him into your heart.

I have learned that it takes a lot of work to be Christ-like and I am still working on achieving it. The devil on the other hand is working 24/7 to send you and me straight to hell. We are in spiritual warfare and the devil knows that his time is getting nearer, so he is working overtime to win us over to his side. Have you noticed that when you are trying to do the right thing, you get distractions from all directions, family, and friends? But when you are working with the devil you get very few distractions, because you are working against God.

God knew that we would have distractions on all levels, so He provided us with the tools to fight the devil. Galatians 5:22-26 states *"But what happens when we live God's way? He brings gifts into our lives, much the same way that fruit appears in an orchard—things like affection for others, exuberance about life, serenity. We develop a willingness to stick with things, a sense of compassion in the heart, and a conviction that a basic holiness permeates things and people. We find ourselves involved in loyal commitments, not needing to force our way in life, able to marshal and direct our energies wisely. Legalism is helpless in bringing this about; it only gets in the way. Among those who belong to Christ, everything connected with getting our own way and mindlessly responding to what everyone else calls necessities is killed off for good—crucified. Since this is the kind of life we have chosen, the life of the Spirit, let us make sure that we do not just hold it as an idea in our heads or a sentiment in our hearts, but work out its implications in every detail of our lives. That means we will not compare ourselves with each other as if one of us were better and another worse. We have far more interesting things to do with our lives. Each of us is an original." (MGS) What* a blessing to know that God made us different, there is no one like us. There is not another person on this earth that thinks, feels, or acts as you do, so your relationship with God is personal and He responds to your needs and wants in a special way.

Ask yourself this question, "Do I want to live my life trying to be a more fruitful Christian or not? You have to answer this question and decide for yourself! Fruitful or Fruitless!

This thing we call life will knock you down and the only thing that can pick you up is calling on the name of Jesus. The faith that you have in God will see you through all your problems, and give you the strength to keep trying. God sent the Holy Spirit to help you and direct your life. We all want to live a good life, but we have different ideas about "What a good life means to us!" What does it mean to you?

Are you ready to surrender everything to God? Well, this is all a part of the sanctification process and it does not happen overnight, sometimes it may take a lifetime. To start we have to open our hearts, minds, and body to the Holy Spirit so he can mold us as he sees fit. Once we ask the Holy Spirit to come into our hearts, we have to be open to the changes that will occur, no matter how painful it may be. This is the start of stepping into discipleship!

CHAPTER 2

Stepping Into Discipleship - Study to Show Thyself Approved

As a disciple you need to know the word of God, so you can't be fooled by false prophets. Study the word for yourself, "God bless the child that has his/her own". In this case, it is knowledge of the bible. If you are going to be a disciple that is bearing spiritual fruit from the Holy Spirit, then you need to know that you have been marked as stated in (Matthew 7:16-20) *"You will fully recognize them by their fruits. Do people pick grapes from thorns or figs from thistles? Even so, every healthy (sound) tree bears good fruit (worthy of admiration), but the sickly (decaying, worthless) tree bears bad (worthless) fruit. A good (healthy) tree cannot bear bad (worthless) fruit, nor can a bad (diseased) tree bear excellent fruit (worthy of admiration)". (AMP) The* Fruit of the Spirits are gifts given to you by God, the 9 Fruits of the Spirit are as follows:

1. Love
2. Joy
3. Peace

4. Patient and Endurance
5. Kindness
6. Goodness
7. Faith and Faithfulness
8. Gentleness
9. Self-Discipline

(Galatians 5:22-23) KJV

Examine your life, do you see any of the Fruit of the Spirit manifesting in you? Let us examine each one!

STEPPING INTO LOVE

"BY THIS SHALL ALL MEN KNOW THAT YE ARE MY DISCIPLES IF YE HAVE LOVE ONE TO ANOTHER". (JOHN 13:35) KJV

You may ask yourself "What does love have to do with it? Well, love has everything to do with it. To be a disciple of God you must love everyone, the good, the bad, and the ugly.

Let's explore some definitions of love from the Bible Dictionary and Commentaries:

- Unselfish, benevolent concern for another; brotherly concern; the object of brotherly concern

- The self-denying, self-sacrificing, Christ-like love is the foundation of all other graces.

- The high esteem which God has for His human children, and the high regard which they, in turn, should have for Him and other people.

God, provides us with many verses on what is found in true love, here are two verses that I like;

1. *"There is no fear in love; but perfect love cast out fear, because fear involves torment. But he who fears has not been made perfect in love".* (1 John 4:18) KJV

2. *"Love suffers long and is kind; love does not envy; love does not parade itself, is not puffed up; does not behave rudely, does not seek its own, is not provoked, thinks no evil; does not rejoice in iniquity, but rejoices in the truth; bears all things, believes all things, hope all things. Endures all things, Love never fails".* (1Corinthians 13:4-8) NIV

There are many kinds of love, but we will examine three, Agape, Eros, and Philia.

First is Agape Love

What is Agape love? Agape is a Greek word that is often translated in the Old Testament to mean love. Agape is unique, it is the kind of love that we get from God whose very nature is love itself. Apostle John stated in (1John 4:7-10) *"My beloved friends, let us continue to love each other since love comes from God. Everyone who loves is born of God and experiences a relationship with God. The person who refuses to love doesn't know the first thing about God, because God is love—so you can't know him if you don't love. This is how God showed his love for us: God sent his only Son into the world so we might live through him. This is the kind of love we are talking about—not that we once upon a time loved God, but that he loved us and sent his Son as a sacrifice to clear away our sins and the damage they've done to our relationship with God." (MSG) Having* a personal relationship with God is so VERY important in our lives and in deciding which road to take on our journey to discipleship. Knowing that God loves you, no matter what you do is a comfort. We may fall in and out of love with our boy or girlfriends, but God's love is everlasting. He will always forgive us and he will never forsake us. God's love, is a love that you can depend on in times of trouble and when everything is going great it's a wonderful feeling to know that you are loved despite of yourself. When we are going through the storms of life, God is there! When we couldn't see the light at the end of the tunnel, God is there to show us the way, when we are grieving and heartbroken and don't know how we're going to make it through, God carries us every step of the way. God's love is perfect, it is called agape love, this is part of the sanctification process that the

Holy Spirit wants us to learn, that we can experience this love with God.

God asks that we love each other the same way he loves us. God gave us agape love because he knew we would not be able to love our neighbor as we do ourselves, without the help of the Holy Spirit. As stated in 1Corinthians 13:3–7, *"If I give everything I own to the poor and even go to the stake to be burned as a martyr, but I don't love, I've gotten nowhere. So, no matter what I say, what I believe, and what I do, I'm bankrupt without love.*

Love never gives up.
Love cares more for others than for self.
Love doesn't want what it doesn't have.
Love doesn't strut,
Doesn't have a swelled head,
Doesn't force itself on others,
Isn't always "me, first,"
Doesn't fly off the handle,
Doesn't keep score of the sins of others,
Doesn't tell when others grovel,
Takes pleasure in the flowering of truth,
Puts up with anything,
Trusts God always,
Always looks for the best,
Never looks back,
But keeps going to the end." (MSG)

Stepping into Eros Love

What is Eros love? Eros is the word used to express sexual love or the feeling of arousal that is shared between people who are physically attracted to one another, as stated from gotquestion.org. Eros love is a necessary part of a healthy marriage. Eros love is what we feel when we see a man/woman that arouses a romantic feeling in us and he/she gives us that warm and fuzzy feeling and we fall in love. Until we get our heads out of the clouds and slowly but surely the feeling of love will fade as we learn more about that person. As long as we are in that romantic stage and nobody says anything to make us angry or mad, Eros love can last a long time. This is not the love that will support a loving and long marriage. For a long and loving marriage, we need to have Agape love mixed with Eros love.

STEPPING INTO PHILIA LOVE

What is Philia love? This is the love we have for our families and friends; this love is wonderful but can end with a harsh word or misunderstanding. This kind of love also depends on the situation when a man and a woman practice agape love, this can create an environment in which Eros and Philia love can thrive. Ephesians 5:25-29 states *"Husbands, go all out in your love for your wives, exactly as Christ did for the church—a love marked by giving, not getting. Christ's love makes the church whole. His words evoke her beauty. Everything he does and says is designed to bring the best out of her, dressing her in dazzling white silk, radiant with holiness. And that is how husbands ought to love their wives. They're doing themselves a favor—since they're already "one" in marriage. No one abuses his own body, does he? No, he feeds and pampers it. That's how Christ treats us, the church, since we are part of his body. And this is why a man leaves father and mother and cherishes his wife. No longer two, they become "one flesh." This is a huge mystery, and I don't pretend to understand it all. What is clearest to me is the way Christ treats the church. And this provides a good picture of how each husband is to treat his wife, loving himself in loving her, and how each wife is to honor her husband."* (MSG)

Can you imagine the kind of world we would have if men would love their wives and cherish their relationship? Jesus tells us in John 13: 34-35 *to love one another as he has loved us. This will take work on our part to love everyone some people are just mean. With people that are difficult to get along with you may have to pray harder, but love them anyway. Jesus didn't like what the people around him was doing, but he loved them despite themselves.*

Are we any better than Jesus? No! But the Holy Spirit can put the love that Jesus has for his fellow man and woman in our hearts. Sometimes we need to search deep in our hearts for this love, a love that is self-sacrificing and unconditional.

Do you want to learn how to walk in the real love of God? There is only one way, invite the Holy Spirit into your heart to release this love into your spirit and be willing to enter into the sanctification process with the Lord. You can start your transformation into the express image of His son Jesus Christ. Once the Holy Spirit begins to transmit this quality of love into your spirit your job would be to learn how to walk in this love with your words and actions. Once you have this love you can walk in the spirit of love and joy for your fellow man or woman. But you cannot do it on your own, you have to have the love of Jesus working in you to accomplish this. What do these verses mean to you? Matthews 5:43-47 states

"You're familiar with the old written law, 'Love your friend,' and its unwritten companion, 'Hate your enemy.' I'm challenging that. I'm telling you to love your enemies. Let them bring out the best in you, not the worst. When someone gives you a hard time, respond with the energies of prayer, for then you are working out of your true selves, your God-created selves. This is what God does. He gives his best—the sun to warm and the rain to nourish—to everyone, regardless: the good and bad, the nice and nasty. If all you do is love the lovable, do you expect a bonus? Anybody can do that. If you simply say hello to those who greet you, do you expect a medal? Any run-of-the-mill sinner does that." (MSG)

It is loud and clear that Jesus is talking to every one of us personally, but are we listening? Jesus is telling us to love everybody, friends or enemy, good or bad, everybody! Love makes a difference in this world. It took years of the Holy Spirit working in my life before I could love and forgive people that had told lies about me and talked about me, but love is powerful! As God's disciple this will be the first test of your faith, for you to achieve.

God does allow us to make U-turns and He showed me how to dodge the darts of my enemies and now I can say to them "God bless you and I'll pray for you" this did not occur overnight it took years and years of God working in my life and I am so grateful to the Holy Spirit for showing me a better way to live.

God, says we are some strange people, we get jealous, we get hateful and we get mad for the craziest reasons in the world, example; I don't like the way he/she walks or talks, he/she think they're cute or who he/she think they are? You can be the nicest, sweetest person in the world, but someone out there will find something to not like about you probably that you smile too much. But God says "pray for people that hate you" He knows that if we hold grudges or dislike someone because they don't like us, this will keep us from being Christ-like and we cannot live a Christian life if we keep that hate in us. Hate is like cancer; it just keeps eating away at you until we can't see God in anyone or anything.

But God says in Matthew 5:44, *"But I say unto you, love your enemies, bless them that curse you, do good to them that hate you, and pray for them which despitefully use you and persecute you".* (NIV) Have you ever had a friend that you loved and believed in and you thought that they loved you to? Then one day you find out that they had been taking advantage of your friendship? What a hurting feeling and it makes you feel used and abused by a person that you trusted. You did not see the warning signs because they were your friend. Some people will easily jump to conclusions without knowing all the facts especially if it is something negative. When it comes right down to it God is telling us to love these people, even love our enemies as we love ourselves. Forgive them and pray for their misdoings, let them bring out the best in you, not the worst.

If we are to act more like Jesus, then we have to learn how to love people despite themselves. We need to have that same agape love that Jesus has for us, for our friends, neighbors and family. Now that we know that love is the greatest of all the virtues and qualities that the Holy Spirit wants to put in our spirit we have to learn how to walk in that love. Exactly the way God wants us to, we have to develop a one-on-one personal relationship with God. If you are truly in love with God then you will spend time with Him reading your scripture, talking to God and letting Him know how much you love Him. You will involve God in every part of your life, a rule of thumb that will help you is to STOP and asked yourself "What Would Jesus Do" before you participate in any negative activities.

Love transcends people, nations and religions, love is truly the universal language of this world and people from all walks of life recognize that it is very powerful. The number one quality that God would like to see in our spirit is love, Oh! Did I say this before? Yes! And I am repeating it because it is so important that you understand. Even non-believers can see the power of love and how it can change people's lives.

The problem we have when God says love your neighbor as yourself is that so many of us don't love ourselves. We have to learn to forgive ourselves for the sins we have committed. We have been physically and mentally abused by friends, family, and loved ones. Many parents make the mistake of talking down to their children telling them that they are no good, stupid, dumb, and ignorant. It's no wonder that our children have low self-esteem and no confidence. We should be building our children up instead of tearing them down and then they grow up to be adults, with low self-esteem and no confidence and they fall into a cycle of abusing their partners because that's what they learned as children. Words hurt, a thoughtless word can harm our children or adults for life. As Christians, we can run people away from Christ with a thoughtless word. As hard as we try to love everyone, we can't do it without the help of the Holy Spirit working in our lives.

As Christians, we know that part of the answer to "Why people can't love one another in the way that God would like from us is due to our sinful natures. Even born-again believers have problems in being able to walk in love, the way God wants us to in our everyday lives. We have problems being able to love our God, our families, our friends, and even ourselves to the degree and to the intensity that God would like from all of us. If we have the Holy Spirit living and operating in us, then why is it that we can't draw more of His love up into our personalities, so we can have more of this quality working in our life?

Is the answer that too many Christians are trying to walk in the quality of love out of their own strength, out of their emotions, and out of their flesh? Our best is not good enough, no matter how hard we try in our natural strength, we need the help of the Holy Spirit!

What is the Answer?

With all of the physical and verbal abuse that goes on behind closed doors in many marriages and families throughout the entire world, many people have had all of their healthy levels of self-confidence and self-esteem knotted right out of them. They don't love themselves anymore, but they also don't even like themselves anymore. After hearing how no good you are, how stupid you are, how unworthy you are, and how you will never amount to anything worthwhile in this life, pretty soon you start believing in the lies of the enemy. And once you start believing in those lies, you will start to lose all sense of your self-worth and who you are in the Lord.

Do you want to learn how to walk in the real love of God? There is only one way, learn how to draw that love from the Holy Spirit. The only way that you can get the Holy Spirit to release His love into you as one of His 9 fruits, is that you are willing to enter into a true sanctification process with the Lord, Then He can begin the process of transforming you into the express image of His Son Jesus Christ.

Once the Holy Spirit starts to transmit His quality of love into the care of your personality, your job will be to learn how to walk in that love with your words and action towards others.

Matthews 22:34–40 states that *"One of their religion scholars spoke for them, posing a question they hoped would show him up: "Teacher, which command in God's Law is the most important? Jesus said, "Love the Lord your God with all your passion and prayer and intelligence.' This is the most important, the first on any list. But there is a second to set alongside it: 'Love others as well as you love yourself.' These two commands are pegs; everything in God's Law and the Prophets hangs from them."* (MSG)

Love Yourself

What a blessing it is when you can love yourself, some people can't see the positive things in their lives that make them loveable. We judge ourselves harder than anyone else would ever judge us. Trying to love others with what limited, imperfect love we may already have operating in us will never get the job done. This is why Jesus sent the Holy Spirit to help us. Once the Holy Spirit starts to work in our lives, then we will be able to love ourselves and love our neighbor. Once God's love starts to flow and mesh into what limited love we already have in our personality, then we will be able to start to love other people in the way that God had initially intended for all of us to be able to do.

The Holy Spirit will help you out in this area if you are open to receiving His help. He will show you who you are in Christ, you are not a nobody, that you are somebody, and that God cares for you and loves you just as much as He loves and cares for anyone else on this earth.

My mom gave me some good advice, she said "Treat people the way you want to be treated" and don't follow the crowd, I found this to be great advice.

"But I say unto you, love your enemies, bless them that curse you, do good to them that hate you, and pray for them which despitefully use you, and persecute you." (Matthew 5:44) **NIV**

Love God!

Now that we know that love is the greatest of all the virtues and qualities, now that we know what love is and what love is not, and now that we know that God wants all of us to learn how to walk in His love. The very first person you should love is God, love Him with all your heart, soul, and body. God wants to establish a one-on-one personal relationship with each one of us and in this personal relationship, God wants you to be able to truly learn how to love Him in your heart and in your soul.

If you are truly in love with God, then you will spend quality time seeking after Him, His ways, His knowledge, and His direct involvement in every aspect of your life. God will become your best friend, your best lover, and your only true loving Father. This is why Jesus is referred to as the bridegroom and we as His bride. This analogy that God is giving us is showing us the kind of intense and passionate love that He wants all of us to have in our relationship with Him.

LOVE OTHERS

Here are four key verses that God gave us to keep us stepping in the right direction!

1. *"You shall not hate your brother in your heart...You shall not take vengeance, nor bear any grudge against the children of your people, but you shall love your neighbor as yourself: I am the Lord."* (Leviticus 19:17)
2. *"A new commandment I give to you, that you love one another; as I have loved you, that you also love one another. By this all will know that you are My Disciples if you have a love for one another."* (John 13:34)
3. *"This is My commandment, that you love one another as I have loved you."* (John 15:12)
4. *"Beloved, if God so loved us, we also ought to love one another."* (1 John 4:11)

The first verse says that if you can't love your brother or sister, then you don't have a relationship with God. In other words, God will not know you if you can't learn how to love your brother or sister in your walk with Him.

STEPPING INTO JOY

Without love how do we have joy? Love is the base of everything, Jesus is perfect love. Can you have a happy life without love and joy? No! Joy is internal, it is shown by the way you talk, by the way, you walk, by the way, you look, and by the way, you feel. When you have joy you feel happy, God wants us to be happy. What does

Merriam-Webster say about Joy, Happy and Happiness? Well, let's check it out

- **Joy** - a source or cause of great happiness: something or someone that gives joy to someone.

- **Happy** - feeling pleasure and enjoyment because of your life, situation, etc. and lastly

- **Happiness** - a state of well-being and contentment.

Life sometimes deals us some heavy blows, happiness can be lost in the wink of an eye, by an ill-spoken word or action from another person, if we let them. You can be on cloud nine and the phone rings, you answer with joy and happiness in your voice, "Hello, Praise the Lord" the other person reply "What are you so happy about? It seems like someone let the air out of you and all your happiness goes with it. Then they start to tell you all about their problems and how helpless they feel. They resent you for being happy and want you to join them in their pity party. Why is it that some people just want to be miserable and can't find anything to be happy about?

Jesus said to His disciples "*I've told you these things for a purpose: that my joy might be your joy, and your joy wholly mature.*" (John 15:11) (MSG) Let us examine the difference between joy and happiness? Happiness is an emotion, and joy is a feeling or state of well-being and contentment. We can't be happy all the time, because God said in Ecclesiastes 3:1,4; *"There's an opportune time to do things, a right time for everything on the earth", "A right time to cry and another to laugh."* (MSG) If we are happy all the time then when does God get a chance to show us that He is God? We have to experience some bad times so God can work His miracles and healing powers in our lives. We desire things to make us happy, a new car or house, that handsome man or that beautiful woman if you could just get them your life would be complete. Well, you get the car or the house or the companion, then after a while when the newness wears off, you are unhappy again. Joy is everlasting, and it is deep in your soul. Biblical joy comes from God, the joy of waking up in the morning, the birth of your children, being able to smell the wonders of God, to see the works of God, to hear, to taste, and to feel what God has made. All of these are blessings from God and what a joy to experience each one of them. You will not begin to understand the meaning of these blessings until you start to lose them. As you get older your hearing and sight are the likely ones to start fading. But with the intimate relationship that you have with God, you will be glad to enjoy what you have left. Having the joy of Jesus in your heart will carry you over the bad times in your life.

The glorious birth of Jesus Christ brought joy to the world. The Bible even speaks of this joy in:

(Luke 2:10-11) *"And the angel said unto them, Fear not: for, behold, I bring you good tidings of great joy, which shall be to all people. For unto you is born this day in the city of David a Savior, which is Christ the Lord"*. (KJV)

The precious life of Jesus Christ brought joy into the lives of many as He healed the sick, and made the physical and spiritually blind to see. He told them that they could have Salvation by having faith in Him. The sacrifice that Jesus made for us by dying on the cross for our sins, brought believers eternal and everlasting joy.

(John 3:16) *"For God so loved the world that he gave his only begotten Son, that whosoever believeth in him should not perish, but have everlasting life"*. (KJV)

The resurrection of Jesus from the grave brought us joy. He proved by this miracle act He truly is the Son of God.

(John 14:19-21) *"Yet a little while, and the world see me no more; but ye see me: because I live, ye shall live also. At that day ye shall know that I am in my Father, and ye in me, and I in you. He that hath my commandments, and keep them, he it is that love me: and he that love me shall be loved of my Father, and I will love him, and will manifest myself to him"*. (KJV)

Joy, Joy, and More Joy!

The Bible talks about two kinds of joy, Psalm 4:7 speaks of God putting more joy in our hearts, better than the happiness that others get from great material successes. Outward happiness comes from pleasant circumstances and good fortune. When we get a new car or the promotion we have worked so hard for happiness covers up discouragement for a short time. It is temporary and unpredictable. When our happiness is based on circumstance we can look forward to an emotional ride, when we are up it is exciting and we feel we are on top of the world, but sooner than later we hit a downward spin into a pity party of discouragement.

Inward joy comes from knowing and trusting in God and is based on His presence within us. It is steady and lasting, this joy defeats discouragement.

Jesus describes inward joy in Matthew 5:3-12, a passage we call the Beatitudes (be-at-ti-toods). He uses the word 'blessed' to describe experiencing the joy that is independent of outside circumstances. Blessed is that calm and secure state of mind that those who trust in God have.

- Jesus says we are blessed when we are at the end of our rope because then we will surrender to God and He can rule in our lives.

- We are blessed when we mourn a loss because then God can comfort us.

- We are blessed when we are content with just what we have.

- We are blessed when we hunger and thirst for God because He brings true satisfaction.

- We are blessed when we care about and take care of others because then God will take care of us.

- We are blessed when we are pure in heart. (This is being free of sin because we have accepted Jesus' payment for it.) Then we will see God working in our lives.

- We are blessed when we get along with others and cooperate instead of fighting or competing because then we discover our place in God's kingdom.

- We are blessed when we are so committed to God that when we are persecuted it brings us closer to God.

Get this joy by following Jesus Christ and keeping His commands. Jesus told His disciples to do this so that His joy would be their joy and their joy would be complete.

What is Real Joy?

Real Joy is a personal thing with each person, what brings joy to you may not bring joy to another person. Real joy is what turns you on! The one thing that all Christians can have joy in knowing is that Jesus loves us and is coming back for us. No matter what problems that we have throughout our day, we can have real joy in the comfort of His love. Ask yourself "Are you putting your whole body, soul, mind, will and emotions into serving the Lord?"

When you lose a loved one, it can become so devastating that it is hard for you to find joy, but we know that grief and sadness will only last for a season. If we allow it, the seeds of tears can grow into new spiritual growth. Our tragedies in life can become a learning experience if we patiently wait upon the Lord to help us grow. As stated in Psalms 126:5-6 KJV *"They that sow in tears shall reap in joy. He that go out and weeping, bearing precious seed, shall doubtless come again with rejoicing, bringing his sheaves with him"*.

Think of it this way, "If I start my day Praising the Lord and end it Praising the Lord then I've had a good day. There may have been problems and heartache, I may have even cried my eyes out, but if I end the day Praising the Lord, then I've had a good day.

"That's Real Joy!"

Having the ability to stand and cope with the problems of life, depends upon your relationship with the Lord.

Jesus states *"Always be joyful. Never stop praying. Be thankful in all circumstances, for this is God's will for you who belong to Christ Jesus."* (1Thessalonians 5:16-18) (NLT)

Stepping Into Peace

Peace, Peace, Peace, we are always asking God to give us peace, peace of mind, peace in our homes, peace at our jobs, and sometimes we just say "Peace Be Still".

Lord! What is going on! A great number of marriages are ending in divorce, the job market is declining and many of us don't know from one day to the next where our next meal will be coming from. The world is worried about the threat of terrorists, well I'm concerned about a different kind of terrorist that operates right in our neighborhood. We never know if we will be carjacked on the way home or robbed at the mall or someone breaking into our homes stealing our belongings or being shot down by the police, for being black. We need peace of mind, so we will be able to deal with the raging storms in our lives. Our peace has been interrupted by the COVID-19 Pandemic. Families are being consumed with grief for family members, and friends.

PEACE IS DESCRIBED AS:

- The presence and experience of the right relationship, a sense of well-being and fulfillment that comes from God and is dependent on His presence, tranquility, rest, harmony, the absence of agitation or discard.

- A state of inner calmness and tranquility, together with a sense of freedom, when thoughts and worries cease, and there is no stress, strain, or fear.

In the Sanctification process, the blessings of peace are one of the main factors that you should get worked into your soul through the Holy Spirit. Without the peace of God operating in your life, you will easily become shaken, or lose faith in the Lord as soon as adversity raises its ugly head.

The Holy Spirit is waiting to give you peace, but you have to ask Him for it. When you receive peace that flow in your mind, body, and soul, it is a peace that surpasses all human understanding.

GIVE ME PEACE

The one thing we all need and desire is peace of mind. We have tried many of the wrong ways to find peace, by taking drugs, drinking too much, or going on a buying spree, to name a few. So do we find peace of mind in doing these things? Yes, but it is only temporary and when the drugs and alcohol wear off our problems are still there. A troubled mind can come from one or more basic conditions, here are three:

- Fear

- Guilt

- Feeling unloved

We can't cure any of these conditions by the things we have, or can get in this life; they are based on our relationship with God, our faith, and trust in the only thing that can give us peace, God! Our relationship with God is the source of both the problem and the solution.

To have peace of mind, you must be reconciled with God. You must accept Jesus Christ as your own personal Savior. He says *"Come unto me, all ye that labour and are heavy laden and I will give you rest. Take my yoke upon you, and learn of me; for I am meek and lowly in heart, and ye shall find rest unto your soul.* (Isaiah 57:21) (KJV)

What is the Solution?

"Be anxious for nothing, but in everything by prayer and supplication, with thanksgiving, let your request be made known to God, and the peace of God, which surpasses all understanding, will guard your heart and mind through Christ Jesus." (Philippians 4:6-7) (KJV)

Have you ever heard of someone pulling their hair out because they have too much peace of mind? No! What can help us to have more peace of mind is to keep good thoughts (1) to truly accept everything, and (2) truly be thankful for everything. You might ask "How can I be thankful for everything? Well, I'm glad you asked, the answer is, engaging in difficult situations is an opportunity for God to demonstrate what He can do for you and to demonstrate the strength He gives you, which surpasses all understanding. God doesn't promise us that He will change the circumstances, just supply a means to get through the situation. He promises us ways to escape, here are some scriptures that can help,

- *"No temptation has overtaken you except such as is common to man; but God is faithful, who will not allow you to be tempted beyond what you are able, but with the temptation will also make the way of escape, that you may be able to bear it"*. (1Corinthian 10:13)

- *"You will keep him in perfect peace, whose mind is stayed on you because he trusts in you."* (Isaiah 26:3)

- *"Casting all your care upon Him, for He cares for you."* (1Peter 5:7)

Peace is a choice you can make in every situation. Making the choice of peace in a situation can take one minute or a month. Understand that the time it takes you to accept peace in your situation is up to you. You have the ability to say yea or nay!

Do not waste time in wondering "should I or shouldn't I?" Days, weeks, months, and years may be wasted in that futile mental debating. Always remember God has His own plan too. Learn from your mistakes but do not brood over the past. **DO NOT REGRET IT!** Whatever happened was destined to happen. Take it as the will of God. You do not have the power to alter the course of God's will. Why try?

Put **God** first in everything, depend on Him in all things. As David say's "God, my shepherd! I don't need a thing. You have bedded me down in lush meadows, you find me quiet pools to drink from.

True to your word, you let me catch my breath and send me in the right direction.

Even when the way goes through Death Valley, I'm not afraid when you walk at my side, your trusty shepherd's crook makes me feel secure.

You serve me a six-course dinner right in front of my enemies, you revive my drooping head; my cup brims with blessing.

Your beauty and love chase after me every day of my life. I'm back home in the house of God for the rest of my life." (Psalm 23, taken from The Massage Bible)

STEPPING INTO PATIENCE

Lardy, Lardy, Lardy, please give me the patience of Job! If you don't think patience plays a big part in our lives, you had better wake up and smell the coffee! Just imagine what would happen if we had no patience, at the store, when someone bumps you with the cart or standing in line and the person in front of you is doing all sorts of dumb things to hold up the line or driving your car and people are cutting in front of you or putting on lipstick or reading a book and almost hits your car. What would you do?

Road Rage, Yea! But let's look at people's rage, just let someone think you are looking at them in the wrong way or they wave at you and you don't wave back. They will try to take your head off. Many people have been killed or seriously injured because someone lost his/her temper over something that was so trivial. No Patience!!

Wait on the Lord!

We serve a God that is very patient and longsuffering. We live in the 21st Century with the right now generation, I want it and I want it NOW! But, we have to remember that we are NOT in charge, we may want it NOW, but when asking God to help us, our timetable is different from the Lord. God works on a much different timetable than we do and unless you learn to wait on the Lord to work things out for you; your life is going to be full of frustrating and troubling times.

When trouble knocks on our door, the first thing we do is try to solve the problem by adding our two cents, then when things are getting out of control and we have royally messed things up, we find ourselves at the end of our rope. Then we cry "Lord, help me!" all the Lord has asked us to do is STAND, BE STILL AND LET HIM WORK IT OUT. Patience plays a big part in waiting for the Lord to solve our problems. The Lord wants us to give our problems, big or small, to Him and by faith, we know that everything will be alright. Patience is the key.

WHAT IS PATIENCE?

The apostle Paul describes patience as longsuffering in the KJV and NKJV Bible (Galatians 5:22 NKJV). Let's look at the definition of Patience in Webster's II Dictionary:

- Capable of bearing affliction calmly
- Understanding tolerant
- Persevering
- Capable of bearing delay

Now Webster define Patience as "The quality of being patient; capacity of calm endurance", also let's look at what Webster says about Longsuffering; "Patiently bearing difficulties or wrongs"

Can we all agree that patience involves waiting, OK! Now, think of all the times you are put in a waiting position! Waiting to get an answer from the Lord, waiting on your husband or wife, waiting for your children to grow up, waiting for a coworker to finish a project that you need to work on, we spend a large part of our lives waiting on something or somebody.

How Do You Wait?

It is important how you wait, is it with a good attitude, or do you wait with a bad attitude? Can people see the steam coming out of the top of your head or do you look so mean that people are scared to talk to you? This is not patiently waiting! Patiently waiting is deciding that whatever you are waiting for is worth your time and you wait calmly.

Paul tells us in Ephesians 4:1-2: *"I urge you to live a life worthy of the calling you have received. Be completely humble and gentle; be patient, bearing with one another in love."* (KJV)

Sometimes God puts you in situations that will help you develop patience. Consider this example: I am married to a pastor and I know that other preacher's wives will agree with me that if you didn't have patience you would soon develop it. As a pastor's wife, you are waiting 75% of the time. For example, we go to the store, mall, or anywhere, and we see some friends or church members. I speak and ask how the family is doing and then I'm ready to go back to the mission at hand, but the pastor needs to know how everything in that person's life is going, how their mother, father, grandma, granddad, children and even the dog is doing. Now, this is not a bad thing, it is a good thing that my husband cares about people, but when you have a limited amount of time that you have to get your household chores done, get back home, cook dinner before a meeting or program this can get on your last nerve and make you want to pull his hair out. You asked yourself this question "How can I get mad at someone who loves and cares so much about other people?" So what do you do? You learn how to wait and be happy in the wait; you will live longer and with less stress in your life. You develop patience!!!

How you deal with waiting is up to you! One lady told me that the way she deals with waiting is she thinks of it as waiting on the Lord. How can you complain if you are waiting on the Lord? So instead of waiting on my husband to change, I think of waiting on the Lord to make changes in me. I wait with eager anticipation to see how God is going to work in my life. Anyway, this Lady does not know the people that I know, they complain all the time while they are waiting on the Lord to work in their lives. You can't complain all the time and think that God is going to make your wait easier. What will happen is that God will send more reasons for you to wait so you can learn to develop patience.

How Do You Develop Patience?

1. You Pray and ask God to help you wait.
2. You adjust the way you think and wait on the Lord in peace.
3. Be thankful. The apostle Paul reminds us: "*Now may the God of patience and comfort grant you to be*

like-minded toward one another, according to Christ Jesus" (Romans 15:5, NKJV) WE can thank him for his desire and willingness to give us the peace that passes all understanding. And for helping us rest in his perfect timing.
4. Some things are better said not'. Hold your peace and pray instead of opening up and venting your frustrations.
5. Don't give up. God will give your patience.
6. Grow in your faith and your relationship with God. Patience means remembering that it could be worse and deliberately looking for the good.

One day I was having a very impatience day, so I asked Jesus to give me patience, what I didn't know at the time was that Jesus teaches us patience by sending problems our way to help us develop patience, well I soon figured it out and I went back and asked Jesus to please stop sending problem my way because I had learned patience. I will never do that again! You got to be careful about what you ask Jesus for because you just might get it!

Patience means expressing the positive when everything in you wants to point out the negative. It's deciding to overlook some irritating things and focusing on what Jesus would do.

Another reason for us to pursue patience is that it's one of God's attributes. When we're patient, we're more Christ-like. The apostle James writes that the testing of our faith produces patience. And patience perfects us and makes us complete so that we lack nothing (James 1:2-4). The next time you are confronted with a situation where you have to make yourself pursue patience, count to 10 and try to think about how Christ-like you are becoming. God Be Praised!

STEPPING INTO KINDNESS

Kindness is also a Christian virtue, and it is so important that Paul calls it a fruit of the Spirit. Kindness begins in the heart; we are not naturally kind to each other.

Helen Brenneman wrote: "There was a man who had a heart transplant. But the operation was a total failure. For the man was a mean man and the heart was a kind heart. His body simply rejected it." Christians can be cruel and probably without intending to be, at times. The Word of God teaches us, that to please God we must develop the virtue of kindness.

A NEW HEART

"I will give you a new heart and put a new spirit in you; I will remove from you your heart of stone and give you a heart of flesh. I will give you a new spirit that is faithful to me. I will remove your stubborn hearts from you. I will give you hearts that obey me. I will put my

Spirit in you. I will move you to follow my rules. I want you to be careful to keep my laws." (Ezekiel 36:26-27)

Ezekiel 4:31-32 says to *"Make a clean break with cutting, backbiting, profane talk. Be gentle with one another, sensitive. Forgive one another as quickly and thoroughly as God in Christ forgave you."* (MSG)

If we receive a change of heart, we can become different people and it will enable us to be kinder to each other.

Growing in Kindness

Wouldn't it be great if we could wake up in the morning and say, "Beginning today, I'm going to be kind, loving, and full of joy". But, we can't rely on our strength, we need to have the Holy Spirit working in our lives, and then we could do all things, through Christ Jesus that strengthen us. For a whole day just be nice, it may hurt for a little while, but if you keep this in your spirit sooner or later it will become a part of you.

Ephesians 5:18 admonishes us to "Be *filled with the Spirit.* "Text *shows that spiritual fullness results in changed behavior.* "Submit to one another" (5:21); "Husbands love your wives" (5:25); "Children, obey your parents" (6:1); "Fathers, do not exasperate your children" (6:4). Kindness is one of the products of the Spirit at work in our relationships.

Is Kindness Part of Your Life?

To explore kindness in your life, you have to find out if you can be strong and still be kind, be smart and still be kind, and can you be kind to yourself and at the same time be strongly dedicated to being kind to those around you? We have to find the power in kindness, the confidence in kindness, the release in kindness, and the type of kindness that can transform our lives. We need to devote ourselves to the development of kindness so it becomes our reality.

Abiding in Christ through the Spirit empowers us to live in obedience to all His commandments. "No influence is so powerful in human society as practicing kindness." Our example will lead others to be kind. Kindness points to the core of what it means to be alive. When someone treats us with the benevolence of kindness and when someone feels connected enough to reach out to us in kindness, we hear the unspoken message of their efforts that we are worth the bother.

Praying for the salvation of others must be coupled with Spirit-empowered kindness if we are to be effective in winning souls for Christ.

Kindness, or the lack of it, makes a difference in all of us. We must be sensitive to the needs of others, showing kindness to those we serve, to friends and enemies alike.

God has so graciously poured the Holy Spirit out on us to manifest kindness. *For it is "not by might, nor by power, but by my Spirit, says the Lord Almighty"* (Zechariah 4:6) (KJV)

Read this poem from an unknown author, slowly so you can gain the meaning and the power from it.

Kindness Begins With Me

Is anybody happier because you passed this way?
Does anyone remember that you spoke to them today?
The day is almost over, and its toiling time is through.
Is there anyone who can speak kindly of you?

Can you say tonight in parting with the day
that's slipping fast,
that you helped a single person of the
many that you passed?
Is a single heart rejoicing over what you did or said?
Does the one whose hopes were
fading now with courage look ahead?

Did you waste the day or use it?
Was it well or sorely spent?
Did you leave a trail of kindness or a
scar of discontent?
As you close your eyes in slumber,
do you think that God will say:
"You have earned one more tomorrow
by what you did today?"

Author Unknown

Stepping Into Goodness

As a disciple of Christ, we must see the goodness in people when they are consistently putting the good of others before their own needs and they should be able to see the goodness in us.

What is Goodness?

Webster's dictionary states that goodness is the state of quality of being good, especially morally good or beneficial. In a sense, it's the quality of having quality. Other words in the word-field of goodness: beneficial, gainful, useful, helpful, profitable, and excellent. Moral "goodness" is grouped with words such as uprightness, virtue, benevolence, worth, value, and generosity.

GOODNESS OF GOD

The Goodness of God is a foundational truth every Christian should embrace.

- *"Oh give thanks to the Lord, for He is good; for His loving-kindness is everlasting.* (Psalms 107:1)NIV

- *How great is Thy goodness, which Thou hast stored up for those who fear Thee, which Thou hast wrought for those who take refuge in Thee, before the sons of men*! (Psalms 31:19) NIV

- *You can't have goodness without God, God alone is good! "And behold, one came to Him and said, "Teacher, what good thing shall I do that I may obtain eternal life?" And He said to him, "Why are you asking me about what is good? There is (only) one who is good, but if you wish to enter into life, keep the commandments"* (Matthew 19:16-17)NIV

We simply can't separate "good" from "God." Here is where our society, and especially our educational system, had better take note. You can't teach values, you can't teach morality, without teaching about God. "Be ye holy," God said, "for I am holy"

We sat by and let prayer be taken out of our school system, what a sad day that was.

Anything that interferes with our nearness to God, our fellowship with Him, is actually evil. And whatever draws us into a deeper fellowship with God is actually "good". When God brings suffering and adversity into our lives, our confidence in His goodness should not be undermined. Instead, we should be reassured of His goodness to us.

Stepping Into Faithfulness!

Great is thy Faithfulness! Great is thy Faithfulness! Morning by morning new mercies I see. All I have needed Thy hand hath provided. Great is Thy Faithfulness!

These words you may recognize from the song, **"Great is Thy Faithfulness"**.

As one of God's disciples, your faith will be tested all the time. The devil will try to find ways to shake your faith in God and he will use anything or anyone to help him.

Our Webster's dictionary describes **"Faithfulness"** as, to trust, have faith in, abide in, loyal, full of faith or trust firmly and resolutely sticking with a person, group, cause, belief or idea, without waver.

How strong is your Faith?

Are you faithful, to God, to family, to friends, and to yourself?

God requires us to be faithful, when we have taken our last breath and we are standing face to face with our maker, will we hear our Savior say *"Well done thou good and faithful servant"*. (Matthew 25:21) (KJV)

What does it mean to be found faithful? Ask yourself these 3 questions;

1. Did I finish the job that God gave me to do? *"I have fought a good fight, I have finished my course, I have kept the faith"* (2 Timothy 4:7)KJV

2. Did I do the job the way God wanted it done? God tells us what to do and how to do it; the Bible gives us the patterns for living our lives and ministries. The problem that we have is that we think that we can do it better. Do you think that you can do it better than GOD? Many have EGO problems. Many have "Edged GOD Out" and substitute human reasoning and personal preference to solve their problems. Do you really think that we can do it better than GOD? I think we need to realize that God is in control.

3. Did I do the job to the best of my ability? Am I working in the WILL of God? Faithfulness means doing your best, there isn't any room for sloppy work, half-hearted

effort or just doing my duty. Too many of the Lord's servants have the "whatever" attitude. Whatever I do is better than nothing. What if God treated us with this same attitude? Where would we be?

Review your answers, did you pass the test?

UNMOVABLE FAITH

Faithfulness is an essential element that each and every Christian disciple must possess in order to get into heaven. *"Be faithful until death, and I will give you the crown of life"* (Rev 2:10)

Faithfulness is what helps us to overcome the world, the flesh, and the devil, resulting in a crown of righteousness.

The author of the Book of Hebrews states *"Now faith is the substance of things hoped for, the evidence of things not seen"*. (Hebrews 11:1) (KJV) Faith according to the writer of Hebrews is composed of two elements:

- Confidence

- Conviction

The meaning of faith is made clearer when this is understood. Therefore, it is confidence in things hoped for and a conviction of things not seen (invisible). Faith has substance which only comes by hearing. Hebrews chapter 11 speaks of Bible characters that showed great faith. If we take a moment to reflect on the lives of Abel, Noah, Enoch, Abraham, Moses, and others that are mentioned in Hebrews, we will find that they exemplified great faithfulness. We can learn from them and apply it to our lives.

God wants us to be faithful to Him and He wants us to stay with Him through thick and thin or through the good times and the bad times. When we are going through hard times we stick to Jesus like glue. But as soon as things start to look better we start forgetting about the promises we made to Jesus. We stop praying and reading our bible and thanking Jesus for being with us. The better things get the more we forget about Jesus.

STEPPING INTO GENTLENESS
WHAT IS GENTLENESS?

Gentleness can be thought of as the opposite of harshness, sternness, and violence. And the confusion grows when we look at the life of Jesus, a life we are to model as His Disciple. Paul wrote to the people in the church of Corinth asking them, "What would you prefer? Am I to come to you with a stick, or with love in a spirit of gentleness?" Paul is asking them; do you want me to beat you into obedience or to love you there? What do you think?

I can only speak for myself, I would respond to someone approaching me in a spirit of gentleness than if they come at me with a stick. I will listen and respond to one whose demeanor is respectful and caring, but if I'm approached by someone who is explosive, harsh, and short-tempered, I may not hear their concerns. If we keep in mind that if we do not want to be responded to or approached in such a disrespectful manner, then we need to watch how we address people. "Do unto others as you would have them do unto you."

Gentleness of God

We simply can't separate "good" from "God." Here is where our society, and especially our educational system, had better take note. You can't teach values, you can't teach morality, without teaching about God, "Be ye holy," God said, "for I am holy". WE need to put prayer back in our school system. Then maybe some of the shootings and killings will stop, pray, pray, pray that the devil gets out of our schools and go back to hell.

After Paul recorded his spiritual fruit list, he wrote to the Church at Galatians **"If anyone is detected to be in a transgression, you should restore each one in a spirit of "gentleness".** Some people believe the only way to stand up for what they believe is to do so with a big stick which can be thought of as a loudmouth or a bully.

Within our spiritual nature rests, the virtue of gentleness. Gentleness is a quality that can lead to discussion, to a resolution of a problem, to coming together, to the acknowledgement of error, to hope in human relationships. In most cases harshness, sternness and violence lead to the continuance of a problem, to division, to stubbornness, to the dissolution of human relationships, and in many circumstances to destruction.

When we live in our spiritual nature we will be gentle with each other, and a part of being gentle is being respectful. God produces gentleness within us; it is a part of our spiritual nature. It is our choice whether we will approach our human relationships with a temper or whether we will handle our human relationships with gentleness. Somehow we need to believe that being a gentle person is healthy for us and for those whom we interact with.

Gentleness is a choice!!
Stepping Into Self-Control

Self-Control is the ninth and last of the Fruit of the Spirit listed by Paul in Galatians 6:22-23, though it is listed last, there can be no doubt about its importance to Christian discipleship. Can a disciple be uncontrollable in his or her life and still be a Christian? I think not!

We see a good example of self-control implied in Proverbs 25:28 *"Whosoever has no rule over his own spirit is like a city broken down, without walls."* (KJV)

Just say "NO"

Saying the words **"Self-Control"** implies a battle between a divided self. It implies that our "self" produces desire we should not satisfy, but instead "control". Jesus says "We should deny ourselves and take up our cross daily and follow him". (Luke 9:23) Self-Control is saying **"NO"** to sinful desires, even when it hurts. Being a disciple of God is not easy. The devil will attack you in every direction you turn. He will even send family and friends to try to make you sin. Can you imagine even your closest friend, wife, or husband can be a pawn for the devil, without knowing what they are doing.

The Christian Disciple's way of Self-Control is NOT "Just saying NO!" The problem is with the word "just" you don't just say "NO" in a certain way. You must mean it … with all your heart. Say what you mean and mean what you say!

The difference between worldly self-control and godly self-control is crucial. How do we "strive" against our fatal desire? Paul answers: *"I labor, striving according to His power, which mightily works within me "*(Colossians 1:29). He "agonizes" by the power of Christ not his own. Similarly, he tells us, *"If by the Spirit you put to death the deeds of the body you will live."* (Roman 8:13) (KJV)

BEING FILLED WITH THE FRUITS

How does the Holy Spirit produce this Fruit of Self-Control in us? He does it by instructing us in the superior preciousness of grace and enabling us to see and savor all that God has for us. There are far more things that we do not have control over, than which we do have control over. Some things we must learn to accept peacefully, yield to, and work our way through. Otherwise, we could find ourselves "beating our heads against a wall" and driving ourselves crazy, trying to control something that is not in our power to control.

Perhaps the supreme irony is when we realize how little control we have over ourselves. We find ourselves enslaved, addicted to drugs, smoking, and to habits created and engraved on our character over years of practice. This discovery can be a devastating blow to the ego. Sometimes we look at ourselves as being right up there with God, but when God begins to come into focus in our mind's eye, and we care about what He thinks about us, then we begin to be concerned about controlling ourselves.

On the surface, being a Christian Disciple appears to be an easy thing to do, but it takes commitment on your part to be more Christ-like and put your trust in Jesus Christ.

Paul writes, *"You, therefore, must endure hardships as a good soldier of JESUS CHRIST. No one engaged in warfare entangles himself with the affairs of this life, that he may please him who enlisted him as a soldier"* (Timothy 2:3-4) (KJV)

So now you have reviewed the nine Fruits of the Spirit to guide you through the ups and downs of life. It's up to you to work all nine of the fruits in your life. Just ask the Holy Spirit to help you and pray, then watch your life change.

CHAPTER 3

Mentoring – Godly Advice

How can we be a Disciple for Christ and mentor to a new Christian? By telling our story! Why! Well, because some children today do not believe that Jesus lives and that there is a God! Part of the reason is that we do not witness for God, we do not tell our story of how God has helped and healed us. We should be shouting from the housetops about how God has saved us. We want people to think that we have always been saved and sanctified and living a God directive life. We need to tell our story about how God pulls us up by our bootstraps and turned us around and planted our feet on solid ground. Children and Adults want to hear the truth, not do what I say, but do what I do. Being a disciple for God means sharing the good news and the bad news with people. Listening to their problems with an open heart, not looking down on them because they are young or old and may not have experienced the things in life that brought you to God, Don't act so high and mighty that even God can't touch you anymore. Let people know that you care and that you have had to go through tough times in your life, but God was there to show you the way and you were lucky enough to have someone that prayed and helped you find your way. We didn't find Jesus all by ourselves there were Godly people that gave us sound advice and we trusted their words that God would help us if we believed.

God needs our help to spread the word that He is not dead, He is alive and well and He is still in the miracle and healing business. I went through a life and death experience and God saved my life, I think God kept me here to tell people that He lives, to tell my story. People need to hear our stories about saving grace, people are hurting and need a friend to help them choose the right direction, someone to pray with them and for them. They need a mentor like you, to help them find their way. Here are some important steps that may help them find the right mentor. As stated on Goins.Writer.com by Jeff Goins "Ten Important Steps They Found That Work" to help you find a mentor.

1. Find someone you want to be like.
2. Study the person
3. Don't ask the person to be your mentor right off the bat.
4. Evaluate the fruit, is this a person that you want to spend time with.
5. Follow up after the meeting
6. Let the relationship evolve
7. Don't check out when you feel challenged.

8. Press into the relationship
9. Ask your mentor for feedback
10. Commit to the process.

Being a mentor is using your life experiences to help someone else. As parents we mentor our children, teaching them right from wrong, trying to keep them from making the same mistakes that we made. We share our experiences, hope, and faith in God, to get them on the right track, we encourage and support them.

Our churches have lost the art of making disciples, we are concerned with new believers learning the biblical and historical practices of the church, not encouraging them to develop a relationship with God first. The root of discipleship is having a relationship with God that transforms our hearts, minds, and behavior to be more like God.

There are levels of growth in being a disciple, let's mention a few, starting with a baby Christian.

Scripture tells us that baby Christians are helpless, they need food, but not meat or solid food. They are easily deceived and their speaking, thinking, and reasoning processes have not matured.

Give them scriptures, so they can understand God's word, starting with 1Peter 2:2-3 stating *"Like newborn babies, you must crave pure spiritual milk so that you will grow into a full experience of salvation.*

Cry out for this nourishment, now that you have had a taste of the Lord's kindness." (NLT)

Then there is 1 Corinthians 3:1-3 which states *"Brothers and sisters, I could not address you as people who live by the Spirit but as people who are still worldly—mere infants in Christ. I gave you milk, not solid food, for you were not yet ready for it. Indeed, you are still not ready. You are still worldly. For since there is jealousy and quarreling among you, are you not worldly? Are you not acting like mere humans?* (NIV) 2Timothy 3:15 states ", *how from infancy you have known the Holy Scriptures, which are able to make you wise for salvation through faith in Christ Jesus.* ''(NIV)

Then they advance to the child stage of Discipleship and as a child disciple, we need to give them guidance and sometimes we might have to correct them. They are still learning and we shouldn't put them in a leadership role, they should be in the role of servants. We lose so many of our disciples, because as soon as they join the church we want to put them in charge of this program or that group and we scare them off. Join Usher Board number 3, join the Missionary, be the chair for our Women's Day or Men's Day, join my group it is better. We load them up with so many responsibilities that they run out of the church and we never see them again. What we should do is put them in a New Members Class, give them time to learn about the church and the people. Assign them a mentor to shield them from the people in the church, until they feel a part of the church. Give them some breathing room. When the disciple is wrong, don't be afraid to correct them Proverbs 23:13 states *"Don't fail to discipline your children. The rod of punishment won't kill them."* (NLT) They need discipline, don't put them down, but explain to them why you are correcting them and back it up with scripture. They must build a relationship with their mentor so the mentor will be able to give spiritual advice. Bible study is very important at this point in the child's disciple life. The next stage is an adolescent disciple. At this point they are beginning to take on responsibilities, they want to make their mark in the church, they want to show people that they are responsible and can make good decisions. 1Timothy 4:12 states *"Don't let anyone think less of you because you are young. Be an example to all believers in what you say, in the way you live, in your love, your faith, and your purity."* (NLT) These adolescent disciples are ready to take on adult roles.

The older women of the church have failed the younger women disciples by not following God's word which states in Titus 2:4-5, *"These older women must train the younger women to love their husbands and their children, to live wisely and be pure, to work in their home, to do good, and to be submissive to their husbands. Then they will not bring shame on the word of God."* (NLT)

CHAPTER 4

Walking the Walk – God's Way

Stepping into discipleship is a decision that you have to make on your own, no one can make it for you, and this is one of the most important decisions of your life.

God made it personal, when He asked us to make disciples as stated in Matthews 28:19 Jesus said *"Therefore go and make disciples of all nations, baptizing them in the name of the Father and of the Son and of the Holy Spirit."* (KJV)

Making disciples not church members, in our churches today it seems like the only thing that some pastors are worried about is putting people in the pews. Then they can say I got the most people, or I have the biggest church, many of those pastors don't know their people, and there is no personal contact or relationships with the people. Are people becoming just a number on a piece of paper? Have the Holy Spirit been taken out of our churches? Have we edged God out of our lives? Jesus said to His disciples *"Whoever wants to be my disciple must deny themselves and take up their cross and follow me. For whoever wants to save their life will lose it, but whoever loses their life for me will find it."* Matthews 16:24-25(KJV) Now there are some great pastors that are concerned about their ministry and their members. They put in long hours taking care of their churches and God is the center of their lives.

PRAYER FOR OUR PASTORS:

Lord, hit them with a large dose of the Holy Spirit, convict the ones that do not have you at the center of their lives. Touch them Lord, so that they talk the talk, and they also walk the walk with you. Lord, touch and heal any member of their church that they have caused any hurt, harm, or danger. Lord, please help them, I asked these things in the matchless name of Jesus. Amen!

It is not easy being a disciple of Christ, the stronger your relationship with Christ, the more the devil and his helper will attack you. If Jesus was abused and beaten, why do you think that you can get through this life without trials and tribulations, being a disciple of Christ you must deny your own comforts, priorities, and even your life, expect to be embarrassed, rejected, and ridiculed? When Jesus was calling for more disciples, He spelled it out as to what you needed to do and how you needed to act. As stated in Mark 8:34-38, *"Calling the crowd to join his disciples, he said, "Anyone who intends to come with me has to let me lead. You're not in the driver's seat; I am. Don't run from suffering; embrace it. Follow me and I'll show you how. Self-help is no help at all. Self-sacrifice is the way, my way, to saving yourself, your true self. What good would it do to get everything you want and lose you, the real you? What could you ever trade your soul for? "If any of you are embarrassed over me and the way I'm leading you when you get around your fickle and unfocused friends, know that you'll be an even greater embarrassment to the Son of Man when he arrives in all the splendor of God, his Father, with an army of the holy angels."(MGS)*

Ask the Holy Spirit to give you grace and strength to stand up to the pressure of the devil. What is Grace? As explained on (learnthebible.org) Grace is God's unmerited favor. Grace is God doing good for us that we do not deserve. In the Bible, grace and mercy are like two heads of the same coin. Mercy is God withholding judgment or evil that I deserve; grace is God giving me a blessing or good that I do not deserve. Because of God's mercy, I do not receive the judgment of God against my sins; because of God's grace, I receive eternal life and a promise of heaven though I do not deserve them. Both mercy and grace come to me through the Lord Jesus Christ.

We have all received God's grace and mercy at one or more times in our lives, and what a joy it is to know that God loves us so much. This is our witness to the world that God is working in our lives, witnessing is one of the most powerful things we can do to bring people to Christ. How exciting it is to see someone being transformed by a miracle from God, only God can touch the heart and make the change to make that person a disciple. Our job is to let the love of God in us shine through to touch others. *"So if you find life difficult because you're doing what God said, take it in stride. Trust Him. He knows what he's doing, and he'll keep on doing it."* 1Peter 4:18-19(MSG)

Jesus wants us to take up our cross and follow Him, what does that mean? It means putting Jesus first in everything that we do and say. Before we make a move, we should ask Jesus if we are making the right move. If we remember that old saying "What would Jesus do?" before we make any decisions, may help us from making a bad decision. In Philippians 4:13 it states that *"I can do all things through Christ who strengthens me."* God gives us the power to endure any circumstance, and He wants us to be content no matter what we are going through. What? How can I be content when I am hungry or my bills are due and I don't know where the money is coming from to pay them? You can be content in knowing that we have strength from the Lord to faithfully endure. There comes a time in your life when you know that God is real! You know that through it all God will be there for you and will help you through any problem you may have.

I have been in church since I was born and it has been a part of my life, at first I believe in God because I learned about God in Sunday School and from family. God became real in my life when my mother died, this was one of the most earth-shattering events that has ever occurred in my life. It was March 5, 1990, my mother died and my life stood still. I was devastated, a friend come over to my house to be with me and as we were talking, she was telling me how she had lost her mother at a young age and how she had coped with losing her mother, she was being very supportive, but I was thinking I wished that she would stop talking because I didn't want to hear about coping with death. I did not want to hear about death and I really didn't want to hear about my mother's death, then I hear my friend calling me taking me from my thoughts, Mary! Mary! "Yes", I said. "Do you know that your left eye is smelling up?" My friend said, I went to the bathroom to look at it. When I got back into the living room with my friend, I could not open my eye, we said our goodbyes, and I went in the bedroom to lie down. I didn't know what to do, as I was lying there I began to break out in whelps all over my body and the palms of my hands began to itch and as I laid there stretching the palm of my hand so hard that my nail imprint was left in my hand. Then I shut my eyes, the good one and I prayed to God, please stop the itching in my hands and if He did, I would be faithful to Him and serve Him until I die! Immediately the itching stopped in my hands and it scared me, so much that I fell into a deep sleep. When I woke up the swelling in my eye was gone and the whelps on my body were gone too. At that moment I knew that Jesus was really real and I would be His disciple for the rest of my life. The other thing that I learned was that I needed to grieve for my mom, I had been in a state of disbelief about the death of my mom. Just a bad dream and I would wake up and everything would be ok! But it was not a dream, it was real and I had to deal with it the best way I knew how, so I cried, and cried and cried until I felt better. That day my faith grew 200% and it is still growing. At this point in my life I have dedicated my life, to Jesus and I have not looked back. I made a promise to God that "For me and my house, we will serve the Lord" and I have tried to live up to that promise.

CHAPTER 5

Stepping into Discipleship

From this day forward, it is up to you!

Keep praying!

Keep the faith!

Keep your eyes on the prize!

Keep a good relationship with God!

Love your neighbor!

And then after you have stepped into your discipleship, go make disciples for Christ!

THIS IS THE BEGINNING OF YOUR STORY!

REFERENCES

1. Scripture's taken from the HOLY BIBLE. NEW INTERNATIONAL VERSON 1973, 1978 by the International Bible Society. Used by permission unless otherwise stated.
2. Personal Disciple making – Christopher B. Adsit
3. Gotquestions.org
4. Scripture taken from THE MESSAGE BIBLE. Copyright 1993, 1994, 1995, 1996, 2000, 2001, 2002. Used by permission of NavPress Publishing Group
5. Answer.com
6. Scripture's taken from the AMP Bible.
7. AME Hymnal "Great is Thy Faithfulness"
8. Bible Dictionary
9. Learnthebible.org
10. About.com "Heart Bypass Surgery"
11. Merriam-Webster Dictionary
12. Holy Bible App

www.ingramcontent.com/pod-product-compliance
Lightning Source LLC
LaVergne TN
LVHW020427080526
838202LV00055B/5064